ARENA

Other books by Dennis Phillips

The Hero is Nothing
A World
20 Questions

ARENA

Dennis Phillips

Sun & Moon Press

LOS ANGELES

Sun & Moon Press
A Program of
The Contemporary Arts Educational Project, Inc.
a non-profit corporation
6148 Wilshire Boulevard, Los Angeles, California 90048

First published in 1991 by Sun & Moon Press
10 9 8 7 6 5 4 3 2 1
FIRST EDITION

©Dennis Phillips, 1991
All rights reserved

This book was made possible, in part, through a grant from the Cultural Affairs Department of the City of Los Angeles and through contributions to the Contemporary Arts Educational Project, Inc., a non-profit corporation.

Some sections of this work have previously appeared in the magazines *California Review, O-blēk, Temblor,* and *Tyuonyi.* The author wishes to thank the editors of these publications.

The author also wishes to thank the MacDowell Colony
for a residency during which Arena was completed.

Cover: Marzia Gate, Perugia, anonymous 16th century painting
Cover Design: Robin Palanker

LIBRARY OF CONGRESS CATALOGING-IN-PUBLICATION DATA
Dennis Phillips
Arena
p. cm. — (New American Poetry Series: 10)
ISBN 1-557713-128-9
I. Title   II. Series
811'.54   91-050130

Printed in the United States of America
by McNaughton & Gunn
Typography by Jim Cook/Santa Barbara

CONTENTS

1
ELECTION

Those are lines this is a city.

Inner approbation.

Lines are a map with no dimensions
less than a city.
Details of landscape then
or sites.
Details and memory. Absorption / resignation.

*

When you come to the place
and it's not really the place.

All the time in the world.

The stones, the views.

Streets haunting.

Say a party with dozens of faces.

Cells divide and reform, combine, emerge,
disappear.

Light and sound waves. Then
yards, dark with dry weeds.

Or sudden adolescence muted by circumstance.

Where love even.

Against a sounding board: streets and brick.
Wet pavement.

Churches, vapors, ghosts.

*

As if a change had occurred
but none of the signs were visible.

Sculptural or lyrical.

One moment much the same as the next:
"How do I get down from here?"

No matter how often they tried to avoid the one way streets.

Or, timed to a fashion, a city, a europe.

Or paint out all the colors.
Replace them with new ones.
Secondary.

And then the streets again;
the same rider on the same bike.

Entered deeply into their conversation
or intruded.

A hundred faces in a gala room.

After a word.

The lecturer will pull up a stomach
from a long funnel of intestinal flesh.
"If I'm not a potter," he'll say,
"you'll see the delicacy of this crucial organ."

Which approach is a synthesis of which?
Do the rude equal the didactic?

Fondest conversations torn asunder.

The stomach and its porous walls
secreting acids and enzymes.

Someone will hear you and you'll walk past them.

Was it hot? Will it be?

Or crepuscular shadow.

Alone in the neighborhood.
Steps before rain.

Your shoes as you see them
your shadow as you.

Eyes that peer though lace.

The moment you forget the other faces.

He put cut fruit on your plate.

You let him fall back.

People gather for a play.   Black walls.   Excitement.

You forget the other faces.

He put cut fruit on your plate; insisted.

You in your anger, mouths agape,
shocked him, dropped him.

You left the room
and ran the scene dozens of times.

A hundred silent faces.

They elect but ignore you.

Instead of towns
one unchangeable, always, etc.

And every night the ocean instead.

Steel sheen off Sligo, silver off Sandymount
grey and gold off Tarbert, green and white off Santa Monica.

So when the voices turn malignant.

A lane leads to a beach where fog
dissolves the crests of giant breakers.
Light washes out white buildings.

The name of your enemy has both consonants and vowels.

2
EXILE

But perfectly random and coastal.

A convention that forgot you.
People, whose names would be dropped.

Would it be an offense to approach them?
They sit there, each one, thinking things.
Eyes so focused. Mouths tight.

Your means of travel extraordinary,
private, even secret.

Or just physically, the restaurant dark,
large windows, south-facing,
overlooking a huge crescent bay; tables
full of families.

Where *any* phrase might come from.

Goddess slept on middle C.

Or a witness in olive drab.

Convocation of members, filial,
although outside the cars pass oblivious.

It would be so bright where they'd send us.

It was she (not it) who didn't come or if she did
it was a careful secret that only she could reveal and only
she controlled and if that's not abandonment then
maybe she *was* there and what I wore, just by accident,
was the uniform of the place so that no one would ask questions.

It was only my time.

20

When suddenly you slice open a belly
or cut off a hand.

A small discretion
an accent   (target)

accepted compression

We counted laps and reports
trusts and comments,
fearful predators and benign ones.

Perfectly random and coastal.

And you sank into a noon
of expectation and history.

Not an annotated history or a homeland
of your displaced hero.

Time then acquaintance.

The dance more appealing without sound.

Light embedded in the devil's name.

A family gathers on hot nights
under a full moon.

If you were alone.

Light, generated not reflected.
Like heat, or lightning.

You hear voices. No weather to propose.
A fire in the distance.

Who gets to carbon first.

Footsteps filtered through parchment.

Conflict of possession.

A convention that forgets you.

And we who assemble. Packed goods carried in.
On shining trays. That oil is pressed
and used, drilled and pumped.

Or arteries which once did not know
and now know, or their brains
or their research.

This would be towns. Congregation.
Human intercourse but first
a person or family then
a bend of river or fertile plain.

And we who gather together.

That far away there'd be a farm. That many farms
and villages and towns and coitus and train tracks,
highways, jetways, shipping lanes, language.

Or a laboratory.
That once none of these now all of these.

Gathered together with faces.
Esteemed colleagues.
Many dozens. Silent spines.

And time, a factor. Time and acquaintance?
Or only time. Then acquaintance. Then
acquaintance and other factors.
History and culture.

A chart.

A captor who disappears
who reappears, who's beyond harm.

And morning because even dewyness can't yield directories;
no neighbors no signposts in other words even if I escaped.

His shudder, my fear, random and coastal, a prelude

But I *fell* asleep and the tunes
were comforting, sappy, despicable.

Or imagined how it would be without a brain stem.

So I fell asleep, dreamed of the O.E.D.

Those captives are shades not marbles.
Or in dreams they persuade you.

Only the difference encouraging.
The dance more appealing without sound.

In this neighborhood cars run static, alone.

"It's because your writing is 'crafty' "

Then they defoliate. Their greatest joy
until blocks and blocks are bare.

The foreground is shadowed by glimpses
populated by things that have been taken.

Phantom sensations.   Lost contact.

The background here.

Or just this day. Where data.

Or he chose the long route because it followed the sea.
Perfectly random and coastal.
It must not be broken off: the ideas, the voices
that repeat as impression. Your moves. Then boredom.

Resolves into a fantasy of travel; of sojourn
in austere hotels, at the headwaters of historic rivers.
Not about popular culture and not not about it.

And counted how many would attend and how many
                                                wouldn't.
Saw the small cards and felt sorrow then elation.
Divided time into pitiful increments
where before the week was whole. The day
a tiny chip, adrift.

The mysterious date an entry
(who gets to carbon first)

sharp voices from muffled rooms
or do the walls cause it?

Only a rhythm. Not the voices but between them.
Phantom sensations. Lost contact.

Then your name. In other mouths.
Are they heat or light?
And when you don't hear them?

Your hero against burlap. Soundless, preserved.

And when they do? Tap out the meter.

These are three dimensions.
Different histories.

Thunder or aircraft.

This all toward clarity
modest, retaining mystery.

Or: tasks to consume time
when time wants to be prolonged.

The mystery must never be in the line.
It is winter. It is 1729.

3
ONTOGENY

Or hit a melancholy moment.
Silence of chrome and light.

You had been asked to deliver the words
and delivered the wrong words.
Chaos, fiasco.

She took a short route. Found lightless
roads and you remembered a landscape of
caverns, upspiked, downspiked
you knew the words for them
but spikes worked fine.

Even if there was light.

*

Her shelf and earlier her room.

When room:
        A new place, so it floats without context.
        A skull, a stuffed bird, a wild cat,
        bone necklace, talon keychain.
        A string of donkey teeth.

And shelf:
    To hold the collection?
    A barren plane?
    The tapered edge of landmass?

If you make it
and it's impossible, or she.

                    *

Only a note, not a rendezvous.

                    *

Even as a little girl, rumping the sky
cute, complete. A picture.

Then from where comes rancor?

A picture: a reliable memory but
nothing's reliable and rancor
or rumor, even a little girl
rumping the sky.

How will we read this then?
Her room? Her shelf?

Her smile disintegrates to weeping
but an adult voice:
"Why did you? Why? How dare you?
How?"

And you know how old you are now.
And she. And her elements
as here

*

Lack of details. But not generic

not sound through a wall.

Your giant shadows.
The explosive personality
of the inappropriate comment.

Not staring at the same image
but eliminating all the extra.

What gets denser commentary
as the subject gets sparer.

And then you calm.

It's not in compatibility
compatibility's a frame meant to induce
something like guilt.

It might rain
but only for a moment.

Your interpretation of friendship.
But no one waited.

A kind of notation, an idea
but only images that don't conform.

We would have done altruistic deeds
but someone stopped us to complain.

Water slowed our steps. We laughed.
It was a whole house.

This question. And your monoxide
sensitive lakeland.

Just impress us with a deep ceremony
boulders pushing against thin soles.

Still water. Full moon.
Impress of mountains (shadow) on
water (shadow)

Just find a way to keep warm
"Each phosphorescent stone"
and any apocrypha. Your eyes
water. You've tried as hard as you could
and yet every answer reverses
with no insulation.

The very *idea* of eating
at a time like this.

Days wired smooth;
a cool smooth palm.

Or you have no idea where they come from.

Just a molecule, carbon monoxide, oxygen, ozone.

A fire?

Where swarms of fish under a surface of oil
where by day ducks and now
by inverted mountains flat, hydrogen and oxygen,
ready to freeze.

A quiet, a silent air.

Your face.   Your idea.

Would it be a conspiracy if you said no?
Changed your mind and they all agreed?
Because once you decide. That's the problem.

Open the box.

Now superimpose streets. Brick streets, built on hills.
Your bicycle won't do. Rob a bank.
What if you rob a bank but change your mind?
What if you take $20,000 but then return it?

Decide on a menu and stand by it.

What about her mother? Wasn't she ill?
Why serve cornbread when it was intestinal?
But once you decide, people will listen.
Even at the beach site, with all the improvements:
They'll listen anyway.

Take a close look at power structures,
integrate them into your life.

The patrol cars on the way won't stop you.
And if they do, tell them it was a car fire.
Tell them the fire chief gave you instructions.
Tell them the car is a shed and you live there now.
Your suit, your posture, the inflection of your voice.

Never look at the corpse.

As if the beach were only a cul-de-sac.
Even so, take any audience you can get.
They'll believe you.

The others will stand away.
They know your decision will protect them.

Memorize the situation. Memorize your corrections.
Invent a text and subtext. Memorize them.

The brick streets are steep.
They run downhill to a cul-de-sac. People are waiting.
On top of the hill there are no gallows.
Are you safe? Whom would they hang?
But there is no corpse.

Her mother walked in and ate cornbread.
Her color was fine.   Each day a little stronger.
Money so unimportant.   Why the fuss?

If the people listen they'll wait near the sand.
Don't go near them.   They'll never believe you.

Dreams like discourse and interrogation.
Couplets with no rest.

You'll hear it.
Because sheetmetal hangs from fine wire,
knocks together in the breeze you make
when you open that book.

Because you'll hear it and the book's
thick pages. Which are foils now. Or paddles.
Because how do they interact with the air?

Because there is no lift, because you'll hear it.
And no drag. But simple frontal force.
Nor that either.

Because you *fear* stasis.

The book so familiar.

The forms your dearest plan.

Because you'll hear. You're here.

Where a hand follows the contour.

Because there is no door.
No metal. No heat.

4
ARTIFICE

What the presage says.
Who it would be.   Before the saint.

Worship of your own erection.
Shrine of tears.   Adornment.

Recall into the future.
An afterlife.   Shorthand.

Not afraid to be beautiful anymore.
A suspension of use.   Vehicle.

Let the daughter arise foaming
from the sea.   Out of her shell.

All protocol breached.
The proscenium is disturbed.
The camera wobbles.
Catastrophe.

Voices erupt from behind.

Was it the surgeon who snapped the bone?

But that island so close.
Animals, lions

you roar, they run

Shallow reefs clear

But your leg?
Was it an arterial view
or an aerial view?

Cool film of water.

Waded across to the island.

The fauna.

Water a shadow.

Nor teeth of the panthers, nor
coral outcroppings.
Cool film of water.

Her ankles.
An aerial view.

So close to the mainland.

If anyone had seen her
today compared to yesterday.

Obsessive about details.
Film of water. Fauna.
Their hidden teeth.

Now as if now were a verb.

That circular parts of the street.
Lenticular clouds invading.

A kind of springtime.
A memory.   Counting the days.

The way distance, anonymous engineer
allowing water to run off to the gutters.

After years of floods.

But time is static.
Territorial.

You've felt it all day.   The seeds
burst.   Polyps blossom in your fish tank.
A cool film.   It's weather.   Ripe,
fertile, round, open.

Then an adverb.

When all about lines.

Graphic?

Central America.   You'll hear this
dictation.

Or linguistic?

The Americas.   EXT.   INT.

There wouldn't be a need for type.
Protocol breached.

How much could they retain
after so many hours?

The Humbold current the Gulf Stream.
Easter Island.   Ireland.

The chieftains.
Not afraid to be beautiful.

Or linguistic.   Of words in a line.
A suspension of use.
Voices erupt from behind.   A vehicle.

That back in time
where violet is distance and beige the ground.
Yarrow stalks unbalance the chair.

They will *not* be quiet.
It is only sorrow.

In whose arms collapse?
Recall into the future.
An afterlife. Shorthand.

The way grass and roots make a star.

Or a plaza, a square of trees.

True: violets from Parma, basil from San Diego,
arugula from someone's back yard.

Nor that sound: Bamboo moving in unison
low pressure fighting the invisible high.

It's what survives. Cast of botanicals only
the chorus. Yarrow stalks unbalance a chair.

Fighting for an area of expertise.
Cult of the personality.
Claiming what is everyone's
as one's own.

An infinite set of varying greys and blues.
The brown grass at the base of the pine.
The letterpress in a cool pavilion.
The fear of electric shock.
A collection of satellite weather maps.

That sound; a wall of giant grasses
pushed by wind.

False echo of footsteps.   Vast field.
Tiled, covered.

Then why the nightmare?
The adding up of others' ages?

In rose desert light.
Ridge and dune.

Where sound.

Where violet is distance
and beige the ground.

Where rain sluices through powder gorges.

You'll never.

Your voice rises against powder and heat.
Who it would be. Shorthand.

5
CONTROL

Would it be the darkness of the scene
or the obsessive behavior of the characters?

That season, where function.

A major distraction.
Was this at night?

Because we count each corpuscle now
each beat, each peristaltic squeeze.
We account for each noticed thing.

That season, each cell.

When ontogeny becomes a real word
when rhythm resonates with meaning.
Or meridians of the body.

Then how dark?
The car ran up a small embankment.
No harm done.

They would not stop their teasing.
Or only their faces did.
Their hands were still.

Seasonal. That's all.

When it was very early in the morning
but the government had ordered the clocks turned.
Light flooded in.

"Let us keep this for you" they seemed to say.
Not the government. Not the characters.

It was, what?
Then a letter came.

And then, but not causally,
an insomnia, where the sleeper
sleeps but agitates.

A captioned, a pinioned phrase,
a literary judgment,
that insulted a friend, used
"fatuous."

When no one will agree.
When the mention of just a word.

What corner was pissed in?

And who was so insistent that
"Changes without notice."

Damp paper gave off salt.

Hands took him into an idiom.

A martini glass
echoing hands and hands
reached him, glad hands, smiling.

Huge zones of pressure
funneled to a pinpoint.

Or a bright red liquid
but clean, not blood, so when the insults come
from the far end of the long table
anesthesia has already been dosed out.

People looked up at him.
What was the custom?
People gathered around him.
But they smiled asking
and took it upon them.
And hoisted him up.
Hi. How ya doin'.

Oil cans floating on the water.

Enforced calm.
Huge tornados of pressure.
And miles under the crust.

He was home.
Under the lampshade
where no hands could glad him.

And those who rescue.
Those who show up unannounced.
Those who hoist and smile.
And those who say *those who*
or call or once upon or
years later.

Those who open the bin
and find grain pouring out from the bottom.
And find themeslves measured by sand.

He didn't know. Doesn't.
Hands held him. Now he drank.
The corporealis no excuse. The flanks of a willing torso.
Hands along sides.
Pointy tongue. Mound of Venus.

Or the narrator who tells of dreams
creates a progression. Voice on paper.
Only the replay.

I mean, who had cut her hair?
Who sat across the table
and remained aloof?
What is the Englishman's proudest boast?
Who was so insistent?
And here sits a conductor
while the captain dozes in the wheelhouse.
Drivers collide with trees
pilots stroke out mid-flight.

When the mention of just a word.

Ten minutes later
police arrived
or the narrator:
Those had been shots
not cars or toys.
This was the city.

And no safe zone.
When the mention of just a word.
Anywhere meant no specific thing.

Folded in paper.

People still walked the street.
That was the custom.
Perhaps some were concerned.
Only the replay.

Offices are ringing
but the workers have left.

No rain. But the wait.

Fog fills the valley.
Green leaves dissolve.
Protected arroyo
dark shadowed.

A few rough lines
but the drawing moves.
Only the replay.

What was the custom?
No one will come in.

Fog comes in.
The helicopters are grounded.

A white light flashes from the town beacon.
No one can receive the warning.

All the footsteps are gone.
Yet the concrete
as if hot from the overheated day.

One mirror, or window, or panorama.

No rain. But lots of humidity.

Each fragment of noise and sound
and sound is noted.

The mirror is nearly a window.
A black room behind.

That would be a memory now.
Her face floats in hands her
open mouth.

Her voice on paper.

But none of this.

Or a calm,
a midnight.
An untraversable distance.
A mirror a window.

"Based on a date or written in smoke"
she said of a reason
she took or mistook.

Knowing that what would come to her
first might be the right thing
or the wrong, she was prepared
to abandon any project.

It is the month of February.
Astrology has seeped into conversations
of all levels.
A thin crescent of moon,
over palm trees and highrises, late.

Or, meridians of the body
of the globe, of the boulevard.

Damp paper gave off salt.
It is the month of June.

6
DIMINUTION

Or singular.
So that your mouth drowns.
And yours too.   It's in a beach town.
Silver.   Treeless.
Why won't they take you?
This is near the border.
The water is cold.

Or then in green.
As if in the midst of something.
As if the etymology of a name.
But also in fog.   A wet sound.

It's only fear that gives such a bad taste.
If they're silent they must be planning something.
The debate will be averted or you'll meet on the stairs.
On a great cushion of moss.   But treeless.

The wall space.   Not rain but drizzle.
The vertical slabs; i.e. humans have been here
and here on sandy lots

where trees won't grow, where metal falls apart,
where shade, where recordings, where meetings,
sun, words.

This is a civilization where these things happen
and where continuity.

The only defining will be done in absentia.

Simple convocation of enemies.
Your foot on their chests. (victory)

"I've always said I understood"

Nor had they offered to pay to enter.

In a temple in a tower in a wall.

Too meek to answer, too tired to delineate.
So why ask again? Why not offer something piercing?

It doesn't matter when anyone calls.

Those decisions and their geography.
Does that answer it?

Or that recurrent street
inclined so that a bicycle.

Peopled by strangers.

What she is giving away to another.

The ocean is rough in a spot
where tractors and earthmovers
herd strings of men.
It is a foreign country.
They build or destroy the street.

There's no use in running scenes over and over.
Why won't they take you?

Only the husks of these matters are real.

The man at the desk gave you misinformation.
The rendezvous could not be made.

There was no music.

Through the empties
to the square you live on.

Because the maps won't work here.
Or that recurrent street.

Cardboard.

Nor the Great Wall
only visible from space.

Through empties
till homecomings

on cardboard
to cardboard

let one thought
on which day.

A root cellar. A mistake in the suburbs;
They miss the labyrinth.

Door entwined.

Pound your hand with a mallet.

You will walk for days.
She says open the door. A root cellar.
It's ivy. An exchange of names.

We have timed the cleansing process:
neither darkness nor humidity.

Cleansing. For example a hand.

Your wet sheets tangle around you.

Or acres and acres
of surging kelp.

Which looks back on itself.

Repeating the conversation before it happens
will activate defensive glands.

Wept and fasted, fasted and prayed.

Which is most comforting.

A litany of advice. Behavior modifications
to overcome.

Color in the night sky, familiar
locales now offsides, a face so intimate
we can't remember.

In livery or in stability.
Neither revenge nor magic.

The ceiling lowered down.
Water is everywhere.

Clothes oft proclaim the man.

You knew you wouldn't be here,
so why do you want to keep me?

Only engines disturb innocent sleepers.

Tell them to neither come nor go.
See how they react.

It is summer, you know.
The sun has been obscured.
Navigation has become confused.
The windchimes move only when the earth quakes.

While the rest of the world fucks
a still, static motor turns.

No: Moisture.

She complained about A and B.
Nothing could be worked out.
The fault could be evenly dispersed.

You are at your best
when your romanticism fades into detachment.

When she refused to
and your vision across town.

Everything comes to an end with biology.
Friends of his parents bought several copies
of his last book.

When she chooses.
And you put that idea aside for a week.

Stairs or lanes.

They read the magazines for the articles
not for the pictures.

Maybe nothing could be done.

*

They had each become attached
in distinct ways, each
to another in the triangle. Nothing
answered the problem.

Luckily civil war had erupted.
You checked your weapon but the battle was
doomed.
When the car looking for Canadian children came
you got in with no remorse.
The driver was certain he could slip you passed the checkpoints.

She couldn't see the difference
but nothing was the same.
The new one reminded her of the old one.

How can it be illustrated?
Men like pictures
women prefer stories.

Water must have spilled.

You face the stern cleric
and demand that he remove the icons
or explain.

Suddenly they were standing,
several of them were wiping the table
or their books.

The weather or the alignment of planets;
Society hitting saturation or a simple acting out.

Water spilled or dry icons remained.
It was *her* religion but she refused to defend the priest.
Her lap was stained and the couch she sat on.

You had accused or confronted the priest.
She was found in the parking lot
setting a pile of wood chips on fire.

A very small amount of water.
A thin, even tide.
Planets or weather, spin of the earth.

You would imagine her later,
you would wonder about the hands that held the matches.

Or all around her faces of saints.

Nothing more comfortable
windchimes stinging the air.

Imposed order. That only mocks chaos.
Tell them it's just another European city
that turns into an arcade.
We've seen that.

We don't cower when thunder rumbles the cell.
Or you made the storm to contrive forgiveness.

The time when everything was for sale.
What's left later? They don't know.

Form: Valediction.
When every third thought.

A sunny yard then.

And sea breeze.

Where nurserymen send you out
on tasks you cannot complete.
Where every Sunday your bowels rebel.

It may not be necessary to defend
the works you love much longer.

When they summon you inside
to watch gifts, what regeneration then?
What is the composition of particulate matter
suspended in the air they supply?

Whether this is political or not.
The same stories. Then, if not political
familiar.

From the outside her hair drawn back.

Figures that appear from a sidewalk beachhead.
They say, "There you are."
and "Don't worry."

A wide plane
down to an erasure of incidents.

So vivid. So irretrievable.

He knew that in each clear moment.

7
DESIGNATION

Though city, not a city
first person peerless
with peers

This toucan too loud
explosive elm
radials outward

that consistant image of summer

On a gameboard you take A
I'll take B
and resist the scale
make it seem or
believe it seems
larger than it is
to keep the inhabitant
off your scent

But it *is* small.

To image the new place.

Startled they look up:
different listening than waiting.

Then: What in the store did they want?
The store a set from an earlier dream.
Even so, how? And the schools,
where did they fit in?
Where would they make their purchases?

What language, though here?

And approval.
Polled the trustees and received permission.
No need to say it twice.

You rushed to a certain concert or lecture
because you had to leave early.

The lecturer or pianist was very old.
He left the stage to thank the woman next to you.
Or she was your wife.

But the road was very stark.
Appointments were waiting in both directions.
Volcanic one way
forested the other.

They wanted you to go to the game
have a drink, relax:
at least half an hour away
this woman might or might not be home.

What was the lecture about?
Or was it music?
What pieces did he play?
The hall was full but you had a ticket.

The island was bare of trees.
Rain was predicted by noon:

Air damp, ground dry.
Was the time printed on the tickets?

The windward is the dry side
or is that the lee?
Or is the lee the windward?

Was she excited by the attention?
Was she a different person listening than waiting?

The stanchions a bridge
supered on your eyes.

This appearance.
What passes.
     .

Not a song.
"Piss on a plate."

A format change.

The stanchion of a bridge
the caisson of a bridge.

The clear versus the channel.
Air damp, ground dry.

Your waiting. Una lagrima.
A tear. Una fica. A fig.

The dream first person present tense
or first person past.
The dream third person conditional.

Or the level of amusement
as a dipstick or thermometer.
I am *amused.*

Was it an airport or an arcade?
Will the computer work when needed?
Shall we walk or drive?
It must have taken place there:
On a train! Where you struck the child.
Will the parents ever forgive you?

Then how shall it be told?

It is only when the publisher expresses distaste
for a series of questions
that the practice becomes questionable.

Then let me stop now.
She held a red felt pennant
representing no country or side.

In an age where neutrality.

At night when the sidewalk is English.
Bold sparrows. Families at dinner.
A wood across the street.
Friends of the family watching T.V.
Do they know?

Or that woman who gave you her breasts,
offered her nipples;
and the car, room for everyone,
even the police don't care.

A wood across the street.
Shades fly out.

Or forms in bathrobes
walking around the block,
plaids, leather slippers.
Do they know?

The wife of a friend
or a friend herself
sitting at T.V. or sleeping
in the car, breasts aroused.

It's late.   The street is dark.
Shall we walk or drive?
Will the police?

Do they know?

Several stories.   Variants.
Were they different listening than waiting?

8
DISPLACEMENT

Nor which step if step is a word
and home if home

where place, Ripa, Gubbio, Sant' Egidio

Each a fortress:
What good's the town if you kill the dwellers?

The world cannot take on the quality of an imagined
scene.

Even the sight of which old friends

Or pulling—no not pulling but
breaking the membrane that holds in English

Picture a mayor who wields power
or a contessa and the power of favors

Coated in soft flame.
The city wall

Pigeons swim through the alley
and the fire sits still.

One day all language will twist into
narrow Etruscan streets and arches
but the pools have been drained.

At the inside hearth.
Music the tendon.

We watch wood change to powder
the flames the comfort blow like wind.
Then seethe.
Vicino il fiume. The need
to prove what?

Never mind that a dead man was hitching
or that an airport is also called a terminal.

You have wrestled with what?

The sleep was round. Stringy noises issued forth.

Called a hobby or accused of a certain style.
But who else could have found a wilderness trail
in the middle of a major "terminal"?

This was only what a signal would have had you think.

How can the officials know what you expect
when they have order forms?

There was a border there.
Someone in the only phone booth refused to leave.
And when no messages can be sent.

The Italian woman cries "horses"
and a medieval quadrant of sky
fills with clouds. Her husband isn't born yet.

If one center of the world has weather.

And at home if home is, say,
the west coast of the United States
or the quietest corner of Saudia.

Faces *and* grammar?

She said nothing is stranger
than the idea of what is strange
400 years later.

She said the weather.
And there were people in her pictures.
The way that ancient city on the hill
is always lit in white.

Or took you home
only because there were certain things
you had to see.

Nor did the shades of certain in-laws
distract you.   They were dead.
They were the better half of politics.

The Italian word for wave is onda.

In each room a rumor
those codes or the desk clerk.

But the view is so intense.
Finally there are stains and walls.
The light so white and blinding.

What a signal would have you think.

But if you *did* tell her.

Or everything we spoke about had different names.

You may bring back a packet of seeds
but some other thing will haunt you.

Invent 20 questions and ask her
and if the veneer is still intact.

Later you'll try in your own language.
The world cannot take on the quality of an imagined scene.

I said the thing but the thing was in code.
And she spoke of the janitor.
What is there and what will come later.

There is a clock but that doesn't count.
There are people in her pictures but who gives a fuck.
There are these *things* but other things intrude.

O, sure, explain how it works.
But we've had it with white noise.
This was only what a signal would have had you think.

Nor the dialogue, unendurable
You were several there
compound (as in grammar)
We might fuck on the road
one as many. Or any.
But that is not domestic.
Hence nothing domestic (fra noi)

Only sleep cures it.
But the rains interfere.

Il suono della mia lingua
nella tua bocca.

Here is the proscenium and your ruins notwithstanding.
There will be a query of a dozen philosophical problems.
Your answers will not count.

Nothing could be more separate.

Or reflexive.
Responses seen in gestures.
But this will separate.   The air is too cold.
The world can not take on the quality of an imagined scene.

That it all goes on continuously.
That none of it can.

Like Giotto's frames
and you float, fixed figure.

Or the tourist who has learned
only one pose for the snapshots.

The power of benediction
because in this frame the buildings don't tilt.

In other words the pace of life
or the belief in an order that has no patience.

It remains true about the retentiveness of brain cells
but that is not where St. Francis stayed.

Retention is a broad subject
where the frames stay very much the same.

If the building tips in the next frame
the woman who killed her boyfriend
will sit calmly on a damp park bench
and inspect her gloves.

The time will be less dictatorial
a plane with skids will land on ice.

Surrounding the field were people speaking English.
This was a shock but it helped to clarify
what country we were in.

Your voice in a room
so far away
pinpoints swarm over us.

From the base
but always from the base.

Then what could I say?
Protect this weather?
Listen carefully
to three chords?

Your voice in a room so far away.
Your list.

There's a time each day
when the birds collide.

The flies will take their rest.
Heat will push away thunder
and lightning push away dust.

When will the pounding stop?
And if that's too loaded.

Because you will only hear it.
If hearing and reading.

So sharp. So sharp and then
all the vistas
but that's not what you meant.

Where in sharp is there constriction?
Or simply where constriction alone?

The Italian woman takes the position
that only by ignoring can we pass these traumas.

Because you will only touch them and then be hooked.

The barriers? The traumas?

But a keen sense or view
of or that something or somethings
is or are expected or needed.

And the reasons against.

Light shifts in the scene we imagine.

Tectonic plates or stairways that don't finish.
Languages in collision.
A missing number. Why would she hesitate?
Like opening the door
and both wishing and not wishing.

The mood. That's the thing.
The dark clouds. The frozen lawns.
Even the sight of which old friends.

A particular stress.
What is known and what is not.
Seeing the plates from the beginning.
Being forced into a new case.
Rubbing along the spine of a different continent.

She called about the steam in her mouth.
The number was missing.

Commencement begins then you
break the windows with your fist.

A distaste for a bland weather
or you speak about temperature
as if it were a moment of importance.

But you can't take everything on
and put everything off at the same time.

Windows are shattered
by the bone thrown too hard
too far by a visiting friend who becomes your agent.

How does this work?
(All distance is cut off by grey haze.)

The idea of a figure is not the same.

*

Your covered hand. The windows are intact.
What we don't take away and what we inherit.

Measuring glass or listening to a voice
that will command you but retreat.
Tapping a seam and opening glass halves.
Is the criticism valid or only a covering?

The call is imperative. The glove
is from an Italian story.
It couldn't have been yours.
And so the edge.

Postpartum.

You tell the Italian woman not to worry
the wound is superficial.

She remembers that Hannibal lost
at Lago Trasimeno. You had eaten fish there.
But your hands were so raw.
Nor the storm on the opposite shore, accruing.

A man had left his farm to the bad son.
The good son was poor but his wife was a saint.
Their child was gifted at something
and brought them fame and fortune.
The bad son lost the farm.

This is only what a signal would have had you think.

9
ESCAPE

He asked the child why she paid no attention
but it was he who had fallen asleep.

The opening up or killing of the censor.
Each reference river.
Like a floating factory but now
the colonies are even smaller and speak.

Is she the one whose hair?
The ceilings so high and stark
the industrial light.

This must be terrestrial.
The door was left ajar
but the house remained.
As if the air mass of late.
As if your openness the censor.

Or my hand suddenly numb
these formulas for evaluation
tenses or cages
this clue is a word dropped
a hankie come hither.

Nor as you had thought
feeding time or lines.
As the skin is pulled off
the fibers are white and dry.

They speak a different language.
I might have known whose name.

The tone of reference.
Or calm sociopathic entrances.
The language.

If it is too abstract or if it's too figurative.
Puerile but what definition would suffice.
As if a story or romance gathered a gravity
then they all felt the urge to conclude.

The world cannot take on the quality of an imagined scene.

OK then I need the time.
A circle hooked on a finger.
Touch this meter. Leave too soon.

Candles. Boxes of candles.
The truck was filled with tallow,
three-cornered hats, bell-muzzled muskets,
third grade study films.

The flame was not work.
But lighting was.

You *can.*
What *did* they speak?

To her room

a system

to lose, precognitive, her
hand and crows
outside.
Powerlines.

They know Wordsworth
but who gave them somnolence.

A gift motor.

To her room we rang
until something said no.
Department stores and feed lots.

A gift, electors.

His face therefore in the mirror short hair
nor he who followed as in tailed
arrested by formal guards
taken away.

But the building so old
collapsing and tearing
no escape

It's late the lights are on

The letters or the remembrances
for example: Because the light is fixed on the wall
the shadow across the room behind the cabinet
is always in the same place.

And if the famous building is only crockery
the earthquake will spare none of them.

And those who drove away to prison.

Was it better to ask them not to remove their hats?
But what if they do remove their hats
and become resentful and bury their anger for many years

and use it against you later
when you're unguarded.

Were firm that is resolved
hair short, staring at yourself

not the one who followed you.

Don't attempt it. Not now. Go upstairs.
Urinate. No one will call for you.
The guards will not revolve around the cabinet.

But what falls? Who's safe?

Predawn by minutes and the lights are still on.

The house awake, every one asleep.

And he who followed you
taken away in the back of a sedan.
His uniform and theirs.

Though they are floating and thus out of danger.

The clouds were low and dark over the ocean.

Or, let's face it, terms will never yield flight.

Then take the distractions out of it
open the doors and forget the utilities.

The cliff was sliced off.
Only the rioters would save them.

Daylight only a slice of blue
across black ocean.

The old building succombs to the tremors.
You are thinking all the way down.

A candle would have heated.

Whisper in his ear.
The terminal shows dusk
through chic and clean architecture.

The secrets of commerce.

Or the platform where officials
grant or deny. A terrible toll.

Whisper in his ear.
Or make an excuse that forgives him.

It was only his job.

In the tent, outside,
under the vapor trail. Under cobalt.

May you pass?

Or the oval levels where offices.

How have they raised children
and kept up a business?

How many degrees for each flame?
They were floating and thus out of danger.

These edifices that do or don't suffice.

Say quietly, in his ear, a red speck,
distant, opaque, glazing the set, off kilter,
in a valise that can't conform to its contents.

The piece of the proud owner
he said and walked into the room.
Or it was a foredeck and the winds.
Reversed compasses or that was lighting.

A teacup ocean incredibly blue.
Caldera but which caldera?
Not bottomless but with a vent at the bottom.

Have the pieces open so that any who enter.
There is a debate to be studied.

The nature of an atom must be brought
into the theologians' equation.

A core sample would be taken
and the captain of the mother vessel
will need to speak neither French nor Geologese.

In this way compression can be both an artistic
and a physical concept.

Take for example the pennant.
Nor a pile of ashes nor burial at sea.
Each reference river.

Make your face as the palm of your hand:
blank and mouthless.

A year.   Then a damp cloth called democracy.

Treatment across the river
to be unopened nor banked each
reference river.

Nor the new architects their roofs like airfoils
you know what that could mean.

It is not like cutting into a cantaloupe
vivisecting any mammal the seeds
are elsewhere.

He said.

The valley the seven hills the hill towns.
Just proceed they will not know what
you wish them to know.

These things. The progressive type.
I swear by the almighty.

Though they were floating and thus out of danger.

There were fragments confessions the river
flooding the river unlevied
at the foot

Define the zone and the forces will be marshaled.

The view will bear me out said he.
Strange hearse said he.

Sacrifice.   And then parts.
Not that chop will play here
but the screaming wind and the contact.
Then evening when all the celebrities.
Even the taste of a drop of it
and childhood pours out.
They report on death and then read
from t.v. scripts that inflame them.
No one validates them yet onward.
Open yourselves.
Caldera but which caldera?

10
SEPARATION

That separation, envy.

On account of the granite or inscription.
Opened in this way to patterns and desires.

Then this will empty the basin
and the clouds will not reflect there.

If moon light. Whose phosphors
the street ended.

Test of wonder.

Who spilled stripes of threads and bifurcated.

The sky then was emitting phosphorus.

A date or a holiday
a light to signal disturbance
as if these markers.

And then imagine a place so far south

To the grey building.
They won't come.
A white plant has been laid in the ground.
It's not too late to be kind.

The side without windows at this time of year
but proof of a decade in that plants and trees.

You'll forgive the deed which names harmony
and you'll remember the long practice
because now we may count.

A name will come to or over you
and voices will converge, delaying, obscuring.

An albino succulent but lush
the way a stick protruding
shows the speed of water.

Water would gather here.

As sorrow. A keystone
would gather or an orator.

An impulse, a service, a deception.

When all points converge and the plane is tilted
and a corner shows an outline and permission
and mystery seems overloaded.

Not edema but a kind of memory.

This is the way they seduce you into joining their forces.
They will remember *your* past.

Some belief will interfere
the lights will signal disturbance
a colony of bats will stream from the windows,
the air will be easy to breath
as if the spacing of columns in a renaissance courtyard
would effect the lungs of a visitor now.

The desert of Zion
you dream in the shape of a glass and an agenda.
The clouds will not reflect there.

Nor the precipice which is the same
as a shield a person might affect
to pretend the world sits back.

Because a tract of Palestine
this moment
when the pillar of clouds
and the pillar of salt.
A name will come to or over you
as voices speak
at the same time.

This is how we will gather.
The sun and the shadow.
Neither pro nor con nor neutral.

If a chorus is selected
or the landscapes taken.
An idea of Israel, in the shade.

You said the collection of marbles
or a pocket of melon seeds in the heat.

You read about the schedule,
the opium groves,
these shades that shine when the sun passes.

11
INVASION

The new town was not predicted.
Was it a brothel or the usual clarity
of the winter sea?

If the revolution had come.
The sense of betrayal
and giving away the belongings, so final
so maybe there was no choice maybe
the vanquished one would understand.

Or there was only an empty room now
and the light was the same as it had been.
The windows still in position.
The paint, the floorboards.
A print had to be replaced or a rain-soaked wall.
A few messages had been left.

From the shore the water revealed
coral sand at the bottom and fish
collected in swarms and couples at the shore
were ready to leave it was late in the day
the blue clear green and the smell of their dryness
and no system would replace them or the water
but the right thing was only a favor or a burden

no others watched them and they weren't the ones to feel
these complaints.

I am writing this on an island in a turquoise ocean
the hurricane lamp is flickering in the tradewind my
daughter is sleeping and only the images.

Neither revenge nor magic.

*

The hunt among them had been cancelled.
Why would no one pay attention?
When you visit the author ask of her works.
The stomach for or against.

From wall to wall only light occupied the space.

Perhaps there is always one who serves a sacrificial role.

They may never pay attention.

The neighbors were oblivious and took all that was given.
The new town was not predicted.

Attention to detail: the brothel
was alluring but the public waited outside.

It was autumn. Cold and clear.

I am an old man stealing from others.
Neither magic nor revenge.

*

On the opening. Or press against me.
It is clear and the air is clear.

On.   The.   Opening.

Or maybe I can't stop.

The light of the hurricane lamp.
The island from where I write these memories.
The shipwreck that brought me here
and the shipwreck that rescues me.

The oak was burned evenly. The customers
were unaware that their first duty
had been replaced by a smoking machine.

You ask yourself whether your indifference
is sublimation or if you are simply indifferent.

The lines are stolen from a character
in the *Alexandria Quartet*. Or perhaps
from the *Tempest*. Or the lines survive a
colonist in polynesia or the mythology there.

An Atlantic or Pacific island.
Mediterranean or Caribbean.

Resting or release point.

Under the acacia then no sun
the swell has shifted and we sail
on wave faces, sailed.

It is a taste a wall of silver
on a field of cobalt the caress
of depth.

Strike anywhere.

Granular night and the caress
of humidity.

The schools of trumpet fish and parrot fish
and surgeon fish that follow us
in a volcanic bowl.

The caress of tradewinds warm
at night.

The salt and then through a corridor of jungle
perfumed with rotting passion fruit
a dark pool, fresh, chilly
poured from a narrow falls.

A blue abyss, constellation of fish.

Sitting on the out crop
by the light of a burning daughter.
It is I in a fish scale
patched and nervous.

The sunset is hot
the eastern clouds black
the palms against them
ignited.

Light lost in the transition to summer.

The words at a party
story in a movie script.

Don't expect us to listen
we've been riveted by the hostess.

She forgives the way drillers have left her land.
Sonic booms lattice the sky.

An impasse and a summer air volume
the pressure passes lower then
a little lower. The remembered park,
The vindictiveness of disappointed love.
Pictured as a single point in history.
Any.

A shoal as in a reef a block
smaller than the incidents that make it and then humors
to see them in that context,
so confused so searching for connections
headed off at the pass.

She found a new place in a new land
and started a new life just like that.
Will the tapes arrive on time?
Is there tennis there?
If you fall from your balcony to the street below
will it be hard?

Tapering slowly. *Disappointed love.*
The servants will hear. They will invent
the stories to surround phrases.

There are fingers that would relax.
The grip is painful.
Somethings cannot be discussed via rhetoric.
The table so crowded with timid faces.
And far away the *disappointment of vindictive love.*

We know the image
and they're not going to let you
say something.

Sleep will evade you
and we know the rules for interpreting the meanings
out of disconsolation.

Nothing can replace the sleep as if a moment
really could be recalled.

You thought this would be a period
of excitement and invention, a swiss-style
chalet with devices you had only dreamed of
your balances confirmed on a moving slope of teflon
a frozen wave perpetually breaking.

I have pulled a string of cloth
over your hipbone
a thousand times.

Waking *and* writing.
You will speak of a certain presence
as if charisma were a misused term.

But you mean a person or spirit
that enters your thoughts or room.

I write this from my island cliff
a lantern on my table.

Someone who is not of my conception.

Entirely you will recant.

Fix this here.   Fill the new canister.

We will remember those who suddenly disappeared.
It is no longer a secret.
Those histories are now too transparent.

What *can* we afford to spend?

Where a year ago.
Having come.   This far.
To make room
for a reader.

Or haunted
by birdsong
in the middle of the night.

Where these pieces.

Taking now what you might need later.
Or not knowing.

The daughter writing by lantern light
while I sleep, a mark on our island.

He turns over or bumps me.

I write: Good news cannot be accepted.

As if subterfuge were invisibility.

Though the wasp you slaughtered
buzzed until dawn.

And your insisting that the air was a shawl.

You had traveled on the thirteenth
after all the systems you disbelieve
again forsook you.

The idea that anyone ever sleeps the whole night
without waking.

Or that you might integrate all your reading
into your writing.

Though it will rain the air will be warm.

"No part of a different world will interrupt," you add,
knowing that the throes will continue until dawn.

And though a voice will likely answer you
or a temperature, or a viscous air

To begin with a caldera, underwater.
This in a breeze to keep the mosquitoes off.

The perfect fatigue fighting waves and currents
tides and neuroses.

Then an earthquake because
even or especially volcanic islands.

From which I write, the daughter who speaks to me
at dinner over lettuce, calls me to the railing
or there is no railing calls me
to an edge an outlook, over lettuce,
where we have come.

But whose daughter?

"I am ineluctably drawn to islands,"
I wrote but couldn't use. She said
"I'm drawn to you,"
but couldn't use "ineluctable."

What the gift would be
despite the convention's confusion.

The swell that travels across the Central Pacific
enters the bay and deposits a wad of rope
onto the shore.

Perhaps irises.

Where parrot fish nibble at the plinth of the island.

Because there is a voice of reason and a voice of control
and a voice of madness and a voice of sand and a voice
of order and a voice of forgetfulness and a voice of
dryness and a voice of iron and a voice of glazing and a
voice of humidity and a voice of salt and a voice of
attachment and a voice of daughter and a voice of father
and a voice of the base of the opening of the remainder
of the form of the stuff of the idea of the island.

You should put the stamps in the stamp box.
But a black pearl is there.

Luckily there are no pictures.
They left before loading.
And now only chairs.

When finally a mourning dove.
And we opened the cask we'd been saving:
It was filled with cloth
or was made of cloth and filled with liquid.
We dressed then, or drank.

I have concluded that what they say about the ozone
is right. Summer is now overcast.
Doors open in succeeding houses, the lids
of trash cans are removed and replaced and somehow
I suspect the worst.

The dress I wore or drank to the ball
(was it a wake?) and it's compressions on my private parts.
The dress I lifted to show you.
We did it quickly (I came four times, you once)
we were late for the vote.

When finally the tide shifted.

Below us the bay and the ocean.

I know where you are when you're sleeping.
I found the letter you wrote.
I was relieved but alarmed.

No sun is left for this season.
I'll speak in generics whenever possible.

And every state will introduce itself
in calm latinate expressions.

When finally the avenue.
The cask they sent to our room.
Every night an orchid on each pillow.
Rum from rain water.

The dream played on the ceiling above you.

Your dress so tight in all the erogenous places.
You lifted it and smiled.
The boat would leave but the launch was delayed.
You came ten times and I twice.
Or was it one and one or twelve and five?

We were gathered there that day.
In a cave we found an albacore.
We cut it open and removed the aluminum.

We placed it, one hand each, on the podium.
No one clapped but on the replay they did
and someone dabbed a tear.

I was going to smooth your hair.

There is a long line and the sun is too bright.
The letters that came burnt your fingers
and I'm just a witness without a name tag.

The conversation is about remote places.
Either the flowers arrived on time
or you have become only an idea
with no real place.

An ebb and a flow as in measurements of mood
or thought, as in expectation and now
put your shades on, the sunbursts will not respect
anyone's romantic desires.

On a day when similar things are said
and those who are now only ideas
conduct overt acts of healing for themselves.

I appear only to assure you that the use
of the first person is nothing any of us
need to hide from.

As if just finding the line would solve the geography.

By the light of the burning daughter.

In the shell of the rising hypothesis
tell us why the exile or who
the daughter.

In a vale by a cliff of a mountain
near a forest on the landmass
through the miracle of geology
to the passing lobes in the lasting brain.

There may not be such a place as an island.

We would not prosper there.
The ships that pass pass on the edge
where the play of horizons.

And we from our vantage.

She might arrive at waking if that line of words
would emerge. It's as though I saw them
and can remember their cadence.

Or when I sleep and she takes her shift
to watch the two horizons touch.
I've heard her then, but dared not look.

Those rollers across the ocean face
ripples from this height.
Arising in the shell of a guess
as if finding a line would solve her.

By her burning.

Or I the daughter, secret in plans.
The courts I will address or the tribunals.

From which shell I shall part the two snakes.
This light on this island.
My father awake in a lantern we grew.

It is a steel pin. Its color
across the vista.

The shops would be closed if we could see them.
But they'd hold a passage if we were there.

Asleep by the cold lantern
he writes my voice
awake in my own fire
I create the world.

NEW AMERICAN POETRY (NAP)

1. *Fair Realism,* by Barbara Guest
2. *Some Observations of a Stranger at Zuni in the Latter Part of the Century,* by Clarence Major
3. *A World,* by Dennis Phillips
4. *A Shelf in Woop's Clothing,* by Mac Wellman
5. *Sound As Thought: Poems 1982–1984,* by Clark Coolidge
6. *By Ear,* by Gloria Frym
7. *Necromance,* by Rae Armantrout
8. *Loop,* by John Taggart
9. *Our Nuclear Heritage,* by James Sherry
10. *Arena,* by Dennis Phillips

Forthcoming in this series

Sentences, by Charles Hartman and Hugh Kenner
Gematria, by Jerome Rothenberg
I Don't Have Any Paper So Shut Up, by Bruce Andrews
Into Distances, by Aaron Shurin
Sundays Never End, by Charley George
Letters of the Law, by Tom Mandel

For a complete list of our poetry publications, please write us at

Sun & Moon Press
6148 Wilshire Boulevard
Los Angeles, California 90048
(213) 857-1115